IMAGES
of America

PARCHMAN FARM
MISSISSIPPI'S STATE PENITENTIARY IN THE 1930s

ON THE COVER: Four men view the sweet potato harvest at Parchman. The man with the three dogs is likely a prison employee, and at least one of the men behind the potatoes is a prisoner. The man in the suit at far left (on back cover) is A.J. "Pap" Tabor, a prisoner convicted of murder and pardoned twice by two governors; he became a part of Parchman's popular culture. (Authors' collections.)

IMAGES
of America

PARCHMAN FARM
MISSISSIPPI'S STATE PENITENTIARY IN THE 1930s

Bryan King and Kate Stewart

ARCADIA
PUBLISHING

Copyright © 2019 by Bryan King and Kate Stewart
ISBN 978-1-4671-2800-1

Published by Arcadia Publishing
Charleston, South Carolina

Library of Congress Control Number: 2017946534

For all general information, please contact Arcadia Publishing:
Telephone 843-853-2070
Fax 843-853-0044
E-mail sales@arcadiapublishing.com
For customer service and orders:
Toll-Free 1-888-313-2665

Visit us on the Internet at www.arcadiapublishing.com

Dedicated to Martha Alice Stewart
February 20, 1898–August 7, 1984.

Contents

Acknowledgments		6
Introduction		7
1.	Vestiges of the Antebellum South	11
2.	Farming for Profit	35
3.	Medical Care	63
4.	Women and Parchman	77
5.	Parchman and Popular Culture	87
Bibliography		95

Acknowledgments

We express our gratitude to Jill Smith, director of the Union County Historical Museum for her support and encouragement; Fred Cooper and Daron Burns of the Information Technology Department at the University of Arkansas at Monticello for their technical assistance with the photographs; Liz Gurley and Caroline Anderson of Arcadia Publishing for their expert editorial assistance and patience; Martha Alice "Aunt Alice" Stewart for passing along the Parchman photographs to her nieces and nephews; the archives at the J.D. Williams Library of the University of Mississippi, which houses the Martha Alice Stewart: Time on Parchman Farm 1930s Collection.

All images are from the authors' personal collections.

INTRODUCTION

Historians venture down a variety of avenues in producing an accurate history of their subjects: paper sources, photographs, and oral accounts. This volume offers a glimpse into the narrative of the Mississippi State Penitentiary, commonly called Parchman or Parchman Farm, through a collection of photographs from the 1930s. Although no one has been able to identify the photographer, internal evidence suggests that many of these pictures were taken in 1933. The Mississippi Department of Archives contains several images that were likely produced in the same time period by the same photographer. Martha Alice Stewart, who served as the head nurse at the prison from 1930 to 1939, brought the album to the family homestead when she returned there after her tenure at Parchman ended. Members of the Stewart family kept watch over the collection until they decided in 2012 to donate the original photographs to the archives at the J.D. Williams Library of the University of Mississippi; those images, along with other pieces of memorabilia, bear the title Martha Alice Stewart: Time on Parchman Farm 1930s Collection. The university archives and the university museum exhibited these materials from October 2012 until January 2013.

Born on February 20, 1898, Alice Stewart was the third child and the oldest daughter in a family of eight children. Despite the death of her father in 1915, she still acquired a post-secondary education. In June 1925, she completed her nurse's training at Gartley & Ramsey Hospital, a private hospital in Memphis, Tennessee, and later that year, was appointed a graduate nurse by the United States Veterans Bureau. She assumed a post at the US Veteran's Hospital in Outwood, Kentucky, where she would remain until April 1926. In 1930, she went to Parchman Farm when Gov. Theodore G. Bilbo, who served from 1928 to 1932, appointed her head nurse there.

From its beginning, the governor of Mississippi appointed individuals to civilian posts at the state penitentiary, typically as payment for political favors. Stewart's family never discerned exactly why Alice received her position; the Stewarts were civic-minded, but they were never players in the political arena. Two more governors reappointed Stewart as head nurse: Martin S. "Mike" Connor, who served from 1932 to 1936, and Hugh Lawson White, whose term lasted from 1936 to 1940. As the head nurse, her duties would likely not differ significantly from those in traditional hospital settings, including setting up schedules for the other nurses, arranging appointments for patients, and overseeing distribution of medication. Since a medical exam was the second stop for new prisoners, Stewart would have likely met newcomers. She also served as an anesthetist for surgeries. With a change of the political landscape in 1939, Stewart left Parchman.

The history of the Mississippi prison system might be characterized broadly as murky and racist: murky because its details seem suppressed; racist because the system sought to preserve and recreate vestiges of the antebellum South. Mississippi gained statehood in 1817; by 1836, the state had authorized the construction of a prison in Jackson, the capitol city. Patterned after the New York State Prison at Auburn, The Walls, as it became known, began operation in 1840 and would stand, as David Oshinsky notes, as "Mississippi's most impressive civic reform." The Walls housed primarily white males. By 1860, the prison provided a modest profit for Mississippi by producing poor quality cotton cloth. This facility predated the formation of Parchman Farm by 60 years. The Civil War, however, changed the penal landscape in the state.

In the aftermath of Sherman's march, Jackson acquired the name Chimneytown. Because of its manufacturing success, The Walls become one of the Union army's targets. Despite the damages it suffered, the prison was repaired enough to house 130 prisoners. In 1867, Gov. B.J. Humphreys noted that the facility had been leased to J.W. Young and Company to speed up reconstruction. Mississippi faced problems: incorporating freed slaves into its society, and housing for criminals.

The state initiated a prisoner lease program whereby state agencies and individuals who had the financial means could contract with the state to use prisoners as laborers. The lessors would pay the fines and court costs of the prisoners and agree to provide food, clothing, and shelter for them. The prisoner lease program only included African Americans. It was intended as a temporary solution for the prison system, but it became permanent in 1876. Historians suggest that the lessors did not always provide even reasonable care for the prisoners. Because of growing corruption in the lease program and complaints by less affluent farmers, Mississippi faced the dilemma of needing to reform its penal house.

As a first step to reform, Mississippi bought up tracts of land in the Delta region with an aim toward setting up several prison camps in 1894. The Mississippi legislature established Oakley Farm in Hinds County, where The Walls had been located, and purchased tracts of land in Holmes and Rankin Counties for other prison camps. The largest land acquisitions were those in Sunflower County. In 1900, the state legislature appropriated $85,000 to purchase nearly 4,000 acres in Sunflower County; these properties would evolve into Parchman. By 1901, African American prisoners arrived at Parchman and began clearing land and setting up farm operations.

In the early years of the 20th century, the political leaders, spearheaded by Gov. James K. Vardaman, designed the ideal correctional institution: a prison farm in the fertile Mississippi Delta that could both turn a profit and preserve the antebellum planter culture.

In *"Worse Than Slavery:" Parchman Farm and the Ordeal of Jim Crow Justice*, David Oshinsky notes that "by design it [Parchman in 1915] resembled an antebellum plantation with convicts in place of slaves." The government reacted with the Jim Crow laws of the 1890s. The ground breaking for Parchman began with the construction of four stockades for prisoners, who began clearing the land in anticipation of setting up farming operations.

By 1905, Parchman had turned a profit in fields plowed and planted from a virgin swamp. The prison population also exploded. Between 1908 and 1911, most of the state's prisoners were transferred to the Sunflower County facility because the smaller prison camps failed to realize profits. The prisoners had jobs assigned along traditional gender lines. Men worked in the fields and tended the livestock, while women saw to laundry, cooking, cleaning, and canning the produce from the gardens. When women completed these chores, they would work in the cotton fields.

In light of their relative skills, the prisoners performed a remarkable feat in clearing the land, milling the lumber, and building Parchman's physical plant. Parchman had both a lumber mill, which came with one of the tracts of land purchased in the original land deal, and brick yard; thus, the facility could provide for most of its essentials.

The prisoners would have likely arrived with adequate skills to clear land and farm; a few would have been adept at construction and woodwork. Experience in manufacturing lumber and bricks was less likely. Most of the first camps, as the housing units for prisoners were called, were built of wood. With the passage of time, more brick structures appeared.

In the first 30 years of its life, Parchman had sufficient barracks for the prisoners. Externally, the camps appeared essentially the same. The prisoners were segregated by race and gender, the majority of which were male and African American. The prisoners also constructed homes for the penitentiary staff.

The superintendent's house was something of a marvel in these isolated backwoods. Constructed in the style of the 1890s, a Victorian mansion stood instead of the iconic columned plantation houses associated with the antebellum years. The homes belonging to other staff members were much more modest. The prison grounds also featured a church, post office, and a train depot. From its beginning, the farm operations formed the backbone of Parchman Farm. The landscape was dotted with barns and pens for cattle and hogs. The prisoners also constructed sheds for farm equipment.

Many historians have painted graphic, painful images of life at Parchman both before and after the 1930s. Children as young as 12 or 13, who were largely guilty of theft, were sent to Parchman and housed with the adult population. Parchman historian William Banks Taylor reports that in 1929, some 302 juvenile offenders were housed with adults.

Some privileged convicts, mostly whites, became "trusty-artisans" or "trusties," inmates who were put in positions of authority over their fellow prisoners. These convicts trained bloodhounds, German shepherds, and beagles as "sniff-dogs" or "kill-dogs." They would then use these animals to track down escapees and often kill them.

Parchman has had a reputation for mistreatment of prisoners. Many reported that guards and other officials often beat prisoners who refused to work or who created disturbances. Some even reported random murders, but many historians report that they did not find evidence to support these claims. The history of Parchman Farm prior to 1940 can be at times incomplete, but the photographs in the Martha Alice Stewart collection present one aspect of Parchman's history in the 1930s.

This pictorial history of Parchman divides itself conveniently into five broad categories: the physical plant as it evolved from its early days to 1940; the farm operations in the 1930s, which were designed to support and sustain prisoners and civilian employees; medical care at the facility; the role of women, mostly employees; and Parchman in popular culture, especially in music and literature. The 1930s represent an important decade in the life of Parchman Farm. The Depression cut deeply into the profits once credited to the prison, and better farming techniques began to emerge. Gov. Mike Connor, who had never been a fan of the prison's management and oversight, began to enact changes. By the 1940s, Parchman had cut a good many ties with the "plantation" system.

Beginning in 1940, one might conclude that little had changed at Parchman. The buildings, especially the prisoners' living quarters, remained in poor condition. Racism, moreover, still prevailed in both subtle and overt forms. The era of World War II, though, brought changes to the prison. Parchman began to rely on agricultural experts for advice on scientific farming techniques, and individuals developed programs to enhance the social and religious culture of the facility with regular worship services. Educational programs were also made available, an opportunity which has continued to grow. The chaplain began a band for inmates, apparently on a larger scale than the one in the 1930s. Interestingly, Parchman had a bookbinding business beginning in the 1960s and replaced worn covers on many of the state-owned textbooks used by public school students.

When civil rights workers arrived in Mississippi in 1961, the landscape took a dramatic turn. Although the Freedom Riders were hindered in their efforts by the vestiges of Jim Crow, they were able to empower prisoners. In 1970, Roy Haber, a civil rights lawyer, gathered statements and filed a lawsuit against the prison superintendent in 1972. The suit charged racial segregation of inmates, use of corporal punishment, punishment of inmates, poor medical care, poor shakedown procedures, inmates with weapons, and an abundance of drugs and alcohol. Federal judge William Keady ruled that Parchman was "an affront to modern standards of decency." The following improvements emerged: racial segregation was forbidden, mail censorship was forbidden, living conditions were upgraded, several older housing units were closed and new ones constructed, existing units were renovated, trusty guards were replaced with correctional officers, corporal punishment was abolished, rules and regulations for inmates were established, formal disciplinary procedures were adopted, medical care was upgraded, and better contraband control measures were adopted. Because of the lawsuit, the Mississippi State Penitentiary entered a new phase in its existence. In some measure, though, the results have been mixed. Routinely, prisoners file lawsuits against Parchman, its superintendent, and the State of Mississippi for abuses, most notably violations of civil rights. Parchman does, however, continue to seek ways to rehabilitate inmates through education and workplace training.

One

VESTIGES OF THE ANTEBELLUM SOUTH

In *The Scarlet Letter*, Nathaniel Hawthorne wrote: "The founders of the new colony, whatever Utopia of human virtue and happiness they might originally project, have invariably recognized it among their earliest practical necessities to allot a portion of virgin soil as a cemetery, and another portion as the site of a prison." Writing in 1850, Hawthorne speaks for the first-generation settlers in the Massachusetts Bay Colony, who migrated to Boston in the 1630s. However, he could have written also for the politicians who conceived of the first prison in Mississippi.

Mississippi gained statehood in 1817; by 1836, the state had authorized the construction of a prison in Jackson, the capitol city. Patterned after the New York State Prison at Auburn, The Walls, as it become known, would stand, as David Oshinsky notes, as "Mississippi's most impressive civic reform." The Walls housed primarily white males because "slaves were punished by their masters and white women were 'virtuous' and 'pure.'" By 1860, the prison provided a modest profit for Mississippi by producing cotton cloth, albeit of an inferior quality. The Civil War, however, changed the penal landscape in the state.

In the late 19th century, the state initiated a prisoner lease program whereby those who had the financial resources could "rent" prisoners to serve as laborers. Because of growing corruption in the lease program, Mississippi eventually faced the dilemma of needing to clean its penal house.

As a first step to reforming its prison system, Mississippi bought up tracts of land in the Delta region with an aim toward setting up several prison camps. The state legislature established Oakley Farm in Hinds County and purchased tracts of land in Holmes and Rankin Counties with an eye toward establishing other prison camps. The largest land acquisitions were those in Sunflower County, the home of Parchman Farm.

The main building at Parchman stood inside the front gate. This building would house the administrative offices, and newly arriving prisoners would be processed here; it was one of the earlier structures constructed. In 1901, Parchman began with four stockades to house the prisoners who would begin clearing land, constructing facilities, and farming the land. By 1905, Parchman realized a profit of $185,000. Records do not give specific dates for the construction of the main building, the superintendent's home, or living quarters for the prisoners, but all of them had been completed by 1917.

The prison superintendent took command of the daily operations of Parchman Farm, oversaw farm operations, and reported regularly to Mississippi's prison board. His role drew comparisons to a plantation overseer. This Victorian mansion was intended to replicate the antebellum plantation house. The superintendent's home served as the signature building at Parchman.

This is a view of the original prisoners' quarters at Parchman; it was one of the first buildings constructed and was likely in place before 1910. Some have suggested that the cupola indicates that the structure is the church. A photograph held by the Mississippi Department of Archives suggests otherwise, because the church on the grounds was much smaller than this building and was used by prison officials. The original property boasted a lumber mill; prisoners, almost entirely African American, milled the lumber and built their housing, a priority on the property. Officially, housing for prisoners bore the name *camp*, but prisoners themselves often referred to them as cages.

This is a typical design for one of the prisoners' quarters. This is one of the few camps with a fence near. In addition to a sleeping area, each of the camps had a kitchen and dining hall; each camp had its own kitchen staff. Prison officials assigned inmates to specific camps according to their primary jobs. One camp, for instance, housed prisoners who functioned as carpenters. The most violent criminals lived in one of the camps, but only prison officials knew which camp it was.

This is one of the more ornate camps. The structure at the top is likely a guardhouse with some sort of a warning system. A guard would live in each of the camps; often, a trusty, a prisoner who had authority to guard fellow inmates, would serve as a guard.

This brick camp is distinctive because of the trees around it. Most of the earlier camps were wooden; by the 1930s, just about all of them were brick. The brick camps replaced the wooden ones because the older structures had deteriorated. All the original camps were destroyed in the 1970s because they had become uninhabitable. By 1917, Parchman had 12 camps for males and one for females. In 1937, the prison had a total of 1,989 inmates, the vast majority of them black.

Prisoners would have both manufactured the bricks and constructed the building. This camp conforms to the most typical style for convict housing. A young prisoner sits in front of the building; juveniles as young as 12 and 13 were housed with the adult population.

Of the photographs of prison housing, this brick structure features cupolas across the roof; they served as guard posts. The dormer windows suggest the arts and crafts movement.

This variation on a barracks suggests that those who designed the structures began to experiment with different architectural flourishes. Palladian-style windows appear over the front entrance, a style not repeated in other camps. Whatever style the camp took, it would feature ample windows and long porches.

The landscape in front of this building shows a commitment to making the camp more homelike. The residents are pictured at the front and show that this is a camp for white prisoners. From its beginning, Parchman maintained both racial and gender segregation. Despite differences in architectural style, the camps were relatively the same. Some histories report that the black camps had poor lighting and cramped quarters.

This photograph of convict housing is distinctive because of the people in the picture. Two children and their dog appear on the bottom step. Two men in civilian clothes stand halfway up the steps. The rest of the men are prisoners; the one in the foreground is a trusty as evidenced by his clothing with black-and-white vertical strips. Prisoners in the general population wore uniforms with black-and-white horizontal strips; women wore dresses with black-and-white vertical stripes. The women made all the uniforms.

This camp design appears to be two-story, although the top story seems a bit low for housing. It may have been built to provide for storage and ventilation. The porch and the windows on the ground floor would help cool the living quarters in the often brutally hot summers. As evidenced by the trees, this camp would be more removed from the central area of the prison. Parchman Farm had few trees on the property. Some have called Parchman a "prison without walls" because it did not feature the high fences generally associated with prisons. Strands of barbed wire were the only fences. Prison officials did not particularly worry about escapes because the terrain made walking perilous.

Parchman provided housing for state employees on the grounds. These staff members would include guards, farm managers, and medical staff. This house features a screened-in porch and is surrounded by a fence. These dwellings were generally landscaped in varying degrees. This is one of the more modest houses, paling in comparison to the superintendent's stately Victorian dwelling. In the 1930s, individuals in the Works Progress Administration, a New Deal program began in 1935, built most of the houses.

This house, in the arts and crafts style, represents another approach to staff housing. This dwelling features both a carport and an arbor. The screened-in porch would be a bonus during the summer. The arts and crafts movement gained popularity between 1910 and 1925.

This staff house is constructed similarly to many of the others with its dormer windows and screened porch. It is representative of many of the houses built from the 1920s and 1930s. It appears to stand near one of the fields. Although these structures have landscaping, it is often neglected.

This staff house appears rather more opulent than some of the bungalow styles; its gables give it a distinctive quality. A man sits to the right.

Two staff houses appear in this photograph. The bungalow in the foreground features awnings to facilitate cooling, and the screened-in porch seems a standard feature of the houses. This house also has a small pool or fish pond in the backyard. The house in the background does have a screened porch, but it seems far more modest than its neighbor.

The original purchase of the Parchman property contained a railroad depot known as Gordon Station. The depot would have been used to transport goods in and out of Parchman. The prison also sold lumber and bricks, manufactured on the property, to other entities in the state. A man and a young boy appear in the photograph.

The Black Bayou ran through the Parchman property. From time to time, the Mississippi River would overflow as the result of spring rains. The flooding would cause other smaller tributaries to fill; the Black Bayou would have been one of those areas. The flooding of the Mississippi River in 1927 would evoke memories for those at Parchman, as prisoners were used for rescue efforts. In this photograph, a number of men appear on the banks of the bayou cooking in large pots. This meal would have been a departure from the everyday meals of meats and vegetables.

This brick structure is one of the guardhouses at Parchman; a state-employed guard, instead of a convict trusty, would be on duty at a guardhouse. Given the structures in the background, this guardhouse may have been the one just outside the main gate, where extra security would be required. It would have been near Gordon Station.

This is one of the auxiliary guardhouses. These smaller structures dotted the fields and other areas inside the front gate. Guards would have manned these stations.

This seemingly isolated brick structure is the prison's only laundry house. A washpot sits outside with a wood pile for washing in hot water. Clotheslines appear around the building. The female prisoners worked in the laundry.

Parchman was self-supporting, so it was designed to provide for all the needs of the community. This building is the shoe shop; it contained all the equipment necessary to keep shoes in good repair, especially the brogans that the male prisoners wore in the fields. A prisoner appears to the right. Prisoners assumed jobs that would match their skills, and shoe repair would have been one of those talents.

Pictured here is a garment repair shop. The women's prisons typically made the clothes in a sewing room, separate from this structure. Prior to 1940, the number of women prisoners was small; the number generally did not exceed 30. Two prisoners appear in the photograph.

Early in its history, Parchman began a brickmaking operation to complement the sawmill, which existed on the property when it was purchased in 1901. Based on the disheveled look of the brickyard, one might wonder if the convicts would succeed in producing bricks. Between 1937 and 1941, they produced 650,000 bricks. Some were used to renovate existing buildings at Parchman, and others were sold to outside vendors.

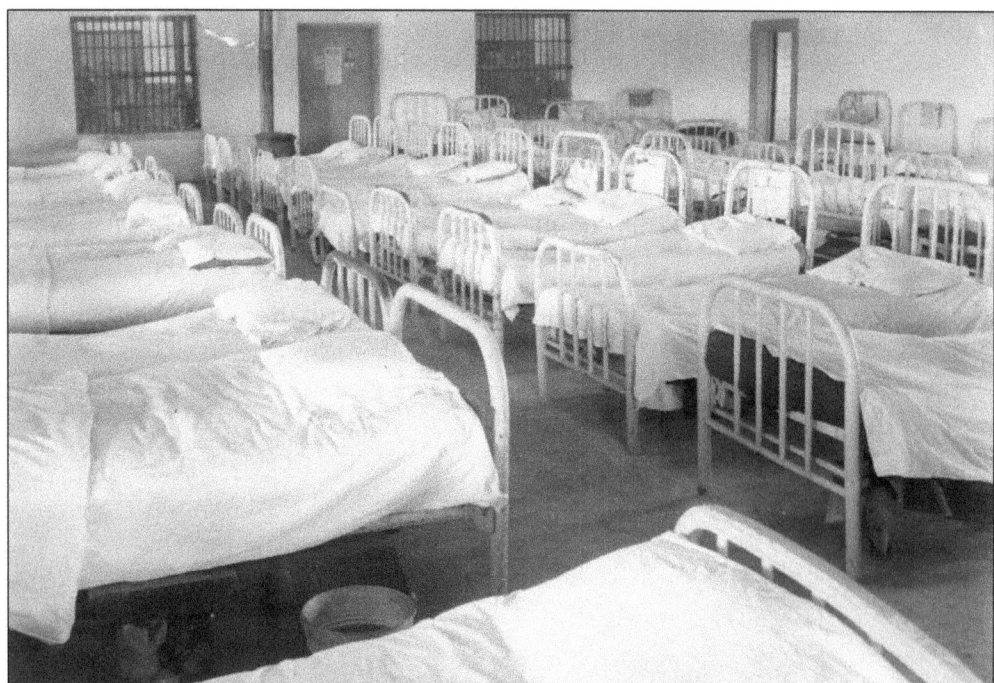

The housing facilities for prisoners might best be described as meager. The single cots are close together, and prisoners would have had little private space. The barracks carried the sobriquet "cages." This term likely referred not only to the physical spaces, but also to the treatment of the prisoners. All the camps did have electricity and running water.

The operation of the kitchen was vital to the life of Parchman. Given the social structure of the penitentiary, those who worked in the kitchen would be deemed the more favored inmates and would have been considered less dangerous.

The interior of the dining facility shows a utilitarian design. The tables and benches were likely built by the prisoners at the sawmill. For ease of cleaning, the tops of the tables were painted. Unlike many of the other interiors, the dining hall does have curtains on the windows and floral arrangements on a few of the tables. The ubiquitous Southern condiment, hot peppers, appears on the tables.

A three-inch snow can paralyze the Mississippi Delta, but an ice storm would have a more dire effect. This ice storm, coating both the trees and the power lines, caused power outages and fallen trees. Even though Parchman was fortunate to have electricity in the 1930s (many rural areas did not), the prison's productivity suffered.

In contrast to ice, the residents of Parchman could deal more effectively with a snowfall, even one of this size. Although convicts would not have to work in the fields on snowy days, they would still have to tend to the livestock.

Pictured is kitchen staff in front of one of the camps. Although these men would have had the primary responsibility of meal preparation, the women would have canned the produce from the gardens for winter provisions.

These prisoners offer some insight into the hierarchy among the inmates. The man on the left is a trusty as evidenced by the vertical stripes on his pants; the ones on the right and in the back were members of the general population as their horizontal stripes show. A prisoner would become a trusty because he had been at Parchman for an extended period of time and for good behavior in following the rules and performing his assigned chores. All of them wear pith helmets, suggesting that it is summer. President of the state prison board Betsy Montgomery worried about prisoners getting sunstroke because of the Delta heat.

This assortment of pistols appears without context. Some have suggested that they were confiscated from prisoners. They may just as well have been firearms used by civilian guards and trusties; the latter group delighted in taunting prisoners with threats of death if they deserted or committed another infraction. Parchman was so isolated that few prisoners actually tried to escape.

This group of prisoners from the regular prison population stands in front of a barracks with a member of the civilian prison staff. Two of them at front left have on chef's hats; one standing second from right wears an apron. They are likely members of the kitchen staff. Even though the barracks and infirmary were segregated, black and white prisoners did interact.

A man stands in front of one of the larger buildings on the grounds. It appears to be the main administrative building. Given his attire, he is likely a visitor from the state government on a routine inspection of Parchman.

These men stand in front of one of the barracks. State officials paid routine visits to Parchman, and these two are likely serving in that capacity. They would visit several times a year to make sure that Parchman remained profitable. They could, for instance, be state legislators who would inspect the prison before acting on requests from prison officials.

This staff house features a small swimming pool in the backyard. The spouse of one of the civilian staff members watches as three children play in the pool. Although Parchman had a reputation for having a brutal environment, guests seemed to come rather frequently to visit the staff.

Because none of the civilian employees at Parchman would have been black, viewers must assume that these are prisoners. Each holds a rifle. The distinct possibility exists that these men are going hunting. Since the prison was self-sufficient, the staff and prisoners had to ensure that there would be enough food for the residents. Prisoners would hunt to augment the food supply.

Well into the 20th century, Parchman was noted for its brutality. Perhaps one of the most disturbing aspects of the prison is that juvenile offenders, some as young as 12 or 13, were housed with the adult population. Juveniles accounted for 20 percent of the prison population.

These prisoners, including three juveniles, are likely returning from the field at the end of the day. Inmates typically worked six days a week for 10 hours each day.

This "Parchman puppy" is one of the breeds of dogs that prisoners and trusties would train as attack dogs to deal with prisoners who tried to escape. German shepherds, bloodhounds, and beagles were the most common breeds used. The trusties enjoyed taunting fellow inmates with threats of dog attacks and shooting if they failed to comply with the rules.

This photograph could have been taken at a dinner on the grounds or a family reunion. It would have been taken on the fringes of Parchman. Parchman provided a house of worship for employees, and prisoners did have access to worship services in the camps. Both the prisoners and the employees could have visitors, and the visitors could come and go with little difficulty. Interestingly, Parchman allowed conjugal visits for legally married males. Before 1950, Parchman offered few recreational opportunities for inmates. On Sundays, many of them played baseball or listened to the radio.

This photograph of a female visitor was taken at the top of one of the guard towers. Parchman's 20,000 acres of flat Delta land would likely have impressed visitors to the facility.

This may be one of the more whimsical Parchman photographs. The picture was taken in front of the screened-in porch of the infirmary. The pants would have been made by women prisoners in the sewing room, which was attached to the female barracks.

This is Black Bayou, which ran through the property. The Sunflower River was also nearby. Barns appear in the background. This photograph dates from the 1930s, when memories of the 1927 Mississippi River flood would have been fresh in everyone's mind.

Parchman had three cemeteries on the property. This photograph was taken at a funeral. Historians found no concrete evidence to support the rumors that large numbers of prisoners died at the hands of Parchman officials. Some prisoners who died at Parchman were never claimed by family, and a prisoner could request burial at two of the three cemeteries. At one time, some individuals complained that the cemetery was too close to the orchard.

Two

Farming for Profit

Driving through the Mississippi Delta, a traveler may be amazed at the seemingly unending fields that run to the horizon. The flatness of the terrain facilitates cultivation and planting of the expanses of flatlands blessed with rich soil. The prisoners who cleared the property at Parchman turned the wilderness of northern Sunflower County into these iconic fields.

Up to and during the Civil War, the Confederate states declared that cotton was king because it was the leading cash crop in the region. Considering that Southern states supplied 75 percent of the cotton to the world, they may have had some justification for this claim. After the war, however, many people still used the sobriquet. In 1895, John Phillip Sousa composed the "King Cotton March" for the Cotton States and International Exposition, which was held in Atlanta. In 1935, the Nat Buring family established the King Cotton Meats brand. Cotton was, indeed, the primary crop at Parchman.

In the beginning, state leaders were less concerned about housing at Parchman than they were with row crops. Parchman resembled a typical farm with its variety of cash crops, especially cotton, along with gardens for raising foodstuffs, barns and pens for livestock, and pasture for grazing. Smaller farms at Parchman functioned liked a bigger farm with the exception that the farmers were not clad in prison garb.

In the 1930s, Parchman could boast some of the more modern farm machinery, but it also still relied on plows drawn by mules to facilitate a good deal of its labors. It faced, as other farming enterprises did, the depletion of the soil that constant planting of cotton produced. The penitentiary was also subject to the same vagaries of the weather and natural predators. All of this coupled with the Depression caused a severe economic downturn at the prison in the 1930s.

A necessary chore in the spring was the clearing of ditch banks, removing dead grass and bushes and reducing the hazard of mosquitoes and snakes. Prisoners cleared the banks of Black Bayou, which ran through Parchman, at least once a year. Because of the flatness of the land, the Mississippi Delta is especially prone to flooding. As these prisoners work along the banks, civilian staff and trusties keep watch.

This photograph offers a closer view of maintaining the banks. The foreground shows that one of the prisoners was in charge of seeing that the work crew had ample water. Interestingly, a member of the staff is being served. Most of the prisoners would be readying the fields for spring planting, so fewer inmates cleared the banks. Two main bodies of water ran through Parchman: Black Bayou and the Sunflower River.

Pictured is a guard sitting atop the bank on horseback. A black dog, trained as an attack dog, sits close by. This photograph offers a good view of the flat land that characterizes the Mississippi Delta.

Clearing the land at Parchman was generally done by hand with scythes and the like. By the 1930s, though, the prison did have some early versions of such equipment as the mule-drawn road grader. The most common use for it would be building roads on the property. When the terrain was flat, the grader could be used for clearing spaces for building new structures and other projects.

Soon after crops had been harvested in the fall, workers began preparing the fields for spring planting, a practice that continues today. Here, several prisoners plow the field using mule-drawn plows to turn over the soil; a civilian farm superintendent keeps watch. Throughout Mississippi, this method of plowing would have been employed on many farms, especially the smaller ones outside the delta.

A solitary worker plows with a mule-drawn plow. The crop is unidentified, but it has clearly reached the end of the growing season. During the growing season from April to October, prisoners prepared, planted, and tended fields of cotton, soybeans, and corn. Vegetable gardens containing such early crops as cabbage, beans, peas, cucumbers, and tomatoes would also require care. This photograph presents a good view of the close proximity of fields to a variety of buildings at Parchman; the ornate house near center contrasts with the surrounding structures.

Cotton was the dominant crop at Parchman, and accounted for a significant portion of the prison's income. After the fields had been prepared and put into rows, cotton seed was planted, typically in May, and harvested from mid-September to mid-October. This field shows the cotton at an early stage in its development. The number and appearance of the plants indicate to the farmers whether the planting had been a success.

One of the first major chores in monitoring the life cycle of the cotton was to hoe the field—a practice known as "chopping cotton." The purpose of this was to remove weeds and, perhaps, thin out some of the plants to ensure the healthy growth of others.

Prisoners head to the field with hoes in hand. Typically, inmates began work at 6:00 a.m. and worked for 10 hours a day, six days a week.

Cotton flourishes during the hot summer months. By the end of August and into September, it is ready to be picked. Prisoners spent most of the day handpicking the crop and putting the bolls into large canvas bags. The bags were most likely made at Parchman by women prisoners.

One of the goals of cotton picking is to harvest as many bolls from each stalk as possible, producing more yields and more profit. In contrast to the preceding photograph, this picking is producing a substantial yield.

The prisoners continue the chore of picking cotton. Mechanical pickers began to replace picking cotton by hand by the middle of the 20th century.

From time to time during the day, the prisoners who were picking cotton would need water. Mule-drawn wagons circulated in the fields offering water to the workers. Dehydration was one of the most common maladies during cotton-picking season.

Clearly, the chore of picking cotton is nearing its end because the stalks contain only a few pieces of cotton. Trying to calculate the number of days assigned to picking cotton is impossible because weather affects the efficiency of the growing season. Summers in the delta are typically hot and dry, but at times, heavy rains halt the harvest. Planting might also be delayed by spring rains and extended cool temperatures.

Pickers emptied the contents of their sacks when they completed a row or when the sack was filled to capacity. From this point, the cotton was loaded onto wagons.

This picture shows clearly the result of picking the cotton clean. Piles of cotton separate a mostly picked field from one needing additional work. In many cases, the prisoners were expected to pick the nearly empty field again. At this time of the year, if the female prisoners had completed some of their assigned jobs, especially canning the produce from the gardens, they would have helped with the picking.

Loading the sacks of cotton onto a wagon or truck was the next step in the cotton harvest. The cotton gin was near the front gate. This load of cotton is parked in front of the depot, which was outside the front gate. Since the fields might be three or four miles from the cotton gin and depot, this truck may have had to travel some distance before reaching its destination.

The wagon of bagged cotton was brought to the cotton gin with mules. Given the historically small appropriations to Parchman from the state legislature, the prison likely had more wagons than trucks.

This conveyance combines both a wagon and a truck for transporting cotton. The tires on the wagon indicate that it would have been one of the newer ones, as the older ones, as seen in the previous image, had spoked wheels.

A mule-drawn wagon with spoked wheels takes another load of cotton to its final stop on the Parchman facility: the cotton gin. When Mississippi purchased the property for Parchman in 1901, the gin was already there. Cotton produced the greatest income for the penitentiary. In Parchman's first year of operation in 1905, the income reached $185,000.

Parchman's cotton gin stood outside the main gate near the depot. Historians have often remarked that Eli Whitney's invention of the cotton gin in the 1790s contributed to the South's losing the Civil War because the region failed to develop industrially, relying instead on agriculture as the mainstay of the economy. In a cotton-producing region, though, the gin would have been a necessity. At the gin, the loose cotton is fashioned into bales for transport to buyers.

Corn was not a cash crop at Parchman; rather, it provided food for the livestock. If sweet corn was not planted in the vegetable gardens, the residents might eat the field corn. The prison may have had some sort of mill to grind the corn into fodder for the animals. None of the histories address the subject, though.

In the cornfields, soybeans were sometimes planted between the rows of corn. This might free up more space for cotton, which produced the most money. The soybeans also enriched the fields.

The mature corn is ready for harvest and is gathered into shocks in the fields. In 2015, Parchman's superintendent noted that the prison devoted 5,569 acres to crop production. By then, Parchman no longer grew cotton, the main crop in the 1930s. The entire acreage of the prison farm from its beginning in 1901 to the present ranged from 18,000 to 20,000 acres. Although figures are not available, the prison probably devoted 10,000 acres to farming.

By the 1930s, Parchman had a corn harvester; this piece of equipment separated the ears of corn from the stalks. These prisoners are bagging the ears. The corn was stored in bins for the winter.

This photograph offers another view of the corn-harvesting process. The corn harvester was attached to a tractor and driven down the rows of corn. Both pieces of equipment were manufactured by Case, which remains a leader in farming. This task would require five or six workers.

This picture demonstrates that the harvesting is nearing its end as evidenced by the flattened stalks around the corn picker. Corn is gathered before cotton, usually beginning in mid- to late August.

Hay was also one of the crops at Parchman. Like corn, it was not a cash crop. It functioned as winter feed for the livestock.

After workers cut the hay, they raked it into piles and loaded it onto wagons. By the 1930s, Parchman did have a hay rake, albeit mule-driven. Since hay provided food for livestock, the prisoners stored it in barn lofts for winter feeding.

This photograph shows hay piled in the fields. Apparently, Parchman did not have a hay baler because the hay is in stacks as opposed to square bales.

Because of the weather and natural predators, any farmer may experience substantial crop losses. At some point in the 1930s, Parchman experienced a significant locust invasion. They ate just about all the crops. As the subsequent photographs show, the corn crop was devoured.

Several locusts have attacked this corn stalk. A locust invasion of this magnitude would not happen yearly. Commonly, massive invasions occur in 7- or 14-year cycles.

Other vegetation did not escape significant damage from the locusts. These plants were destroyed to the point that one can scarce identify them; given their height, they are likely soybean plants.

Locusts caused unbelievable devastation to crops, leaving little to nothing for cattle feed. Since the corn was nearing harvest in late summer, fields could not be replanted.

One of the civilian staff members surveys the damage caused by the locust invasion.

After the locust devastation, Parchman did manage to save a few shocks of corn. From a field this size, the prison would have expected a stronger yield.

This picture shows the total loss of corn. After this, Parchman faced serious problems, especially regarding feeding the livestock in winter. The prison may have had to purchase feed from outside, which would have cut down on profits. This locust invasion was particularly serious because Mississippi was still in the throes of the Depression.

The prisoners would have performed most of their hoeing chores in the cotton fields. They also tended to the vegetable gardens, which contained beans, peas, onions, cabbage, and other food for human consumption. Here, a group of prisoners appear to be weeding and thinning collards or some other Southern greens, primarily turnip and mustard.

These prisoners are working in another garden. Parchman residents knew the farm-to-table concept. Some historians suggest that the abundance of fresh vegetables resulted in a healthy diet for the residents at the prison.

Several prisoners are harvesting sweet potatoes. This photograph also shows one of the guardhouses sprinkled about the landscape. A trusty, one of the prisoners who served as guards, would have manned such a facility.

This is an early vegetable crop, likely green beans, after harvest. The hogs have been turned into the field, where they would take care of removing the stalks. The residents at Parchman would have had fresh green beans as a staple of a spring and early summer diet. The crop was also large enough for beans to be canned for winter consumption. Women prisoners would have likely tended to this chore.

Parchman had a successful pumpkin crop in 1933. Many would consider this large pumpkin a prize. To achieve one of this size, the smaller pumpkins would have been removed from the vine so that all the nutrients could go into one. The man pictured may be A.J. "Pap" Tabor, who rejected pardons from two governors because Parchman provided him with an apartment in the infirmary and reasonably good food. He could also go fishing every day. Tabor declared, "You just can't beat this place for comfort."

Although it was a correctional institution, Parchman resembled any other working farm in Mississippi and boasted livestock. Its barn is a typical design for such a structure; notably, though, it is brick, which means that it was one of the newer buildings at Parchman. Wooden buildings characterized the early days of the prison, but brick structures become more common after 1917. The main section of the barn would have likely had several small indoor stalls for livestock, especially calves and colts. It might have also had some areas for milking cows. On the left, a small storage area appears; often it would be used for corn. Hay was stored in the upper level; when it was brought in from the field, it was put in through the upper door.

Parchman had a large population of mules that were used for fieldwork. Apparently, though, the prison also sold mules to the public. This photograph was likely taken before the visitors had arrived for a sale.

This view of the mule sale gives a sense of place for the transactions. The house in the background appears to be the superintendent's mansion. Since it stood immediately inside the front gate, it would provide a good backdrop for the mule sale. Prisoners and visitors often intermingled freely on the grounds.

The crowd has begun to arrive for the sale. The men in suits may be state employees or locals, since employees at Parkman generally wore cotton shirts and slacks.

This image shows only the Parchman officials, prisoners, and mules. At one time, Parchman purchased 750 mules in Fort Worth, Texas. Because of the Depression, prison officials may have conducted the mule sale to generate income. Also, Parchman had acquired more farm machinery, thus eliminating the need for a large number of mules.

Cattle were included in the livestock holdings at Parchman. They likely provided food in the form of meat as well as milk. The prison may have also sold cattle from time to time as a revenue source.

A prisoner tends a group of hogs. The primary use for the hogs was to provide food and cooking fat. Again, Parchman may have sold some hogs as income.

This prisoner shows off one of the larger hogs. By the 1930s, many of the structures were in ill repair because of strained finances.

Two prisoners, one a member of the regular population (left) and the other a trusty (right), stand with a visitor, as evidenced by the car in the background. If Parchman did in fact sell hogs, this man may well have been a potential customer.

The ultimate fate of many of the hogs at Parchman was slaughter. A prison employee and a prisoner stand by a number of skinned and scraped swine.

A prisoner with an apron stands in a wagon near several hogs. An unidentified woman (left) is probably the spouse of one of the prison employees. The prisoners took charge of the slaughters. They also butchered the meat and rendered the fat. Pork was a staple at Parchman.

Another food source for Parchman was fish. Both the Black Bayou and the Sunflower River were accessible for fishing. Since each camp had its own dining room and kitchen, this group of prisoners may have provided a meal for their camp.

Three

MEDICAL CARE

Despite the fact that prisoners are incarcerated for breaking laws, some even guilty of the most heinous crimes, they do not go without basic medical care. One historian of Parchman denigrates the care that the inmates received and mentions that the infirmary was in extremely poor condition by the 1930s.

The medical community has also used prison populations as human guinea pigs. Dr. Jonas Salk, for instance, sought permission to test polio vaccines on prisoners. Parchman Farm can be added to the list of experimentation facilities. Because of their typical diet, Southerners have been more susceptible to various disorders. In many ways, lard was a staple of life; even healthy vegetables could be made suspect when cooked in rendered pork fat. Fruits were usually reserved as Christmas treats.

The primary function of the infirmary was to monitor the daily medical needs of the Parchman community. Farm accidents naturally occurred from time to time, and prisoners sometimes resorted to violence, resulting in gun and knife wounds. More serious conditions might require surgeries, which the staff could perform. A verbal account of a surgery in the 1930s would, at first glance, appear to evince the notion that the medical staff cared little for the patients. Supposedly, a news story reported that the doctors, for some reason, decided to just let a prisoner die rather than complete the surgery. Alice Stewart, one of the nurses, refused to allow the surgery to cease. The doctors relented, completed the surgery, and the patient survived.

The medical staff got their jobs in the same manner as other prison employees: by political appointment. Although the sitting governors would entertain suggestions from others, they chose individuals at their pleasure. During the 1930s, many members of the staff had been appointed by Gov. Theodore G. Bilbo. Since he was a ladies' man, some have speculated that the nursing staff at the infirmary contained a significant number of attractive woman.

The Parchman Infirmary was constructed with bricks made at the prison. Several historians have commented that the infirmary was in a deplorable condition due to its physical structure and limited medical equipment. Parchman only had one infirmary; the brick structure pictured in the Martha Alice Stewart collection replaced the original building around 1917. It continued in use until a new facility replaced it in the early 1950s.

The Parchman Infirmary stands in a snow-covered landscape. This photograph gives a good sense of the infirmary's location in regard to other buildings; it was located inside the front gate. The nurses would have lived on the grounds, most likely in rooms in the infirmary. If a nurse happened to be married, she would have resided in one of the bungalows constructed for other employees and their families. Parchman employed at least five nurses and three doctors in 1933.

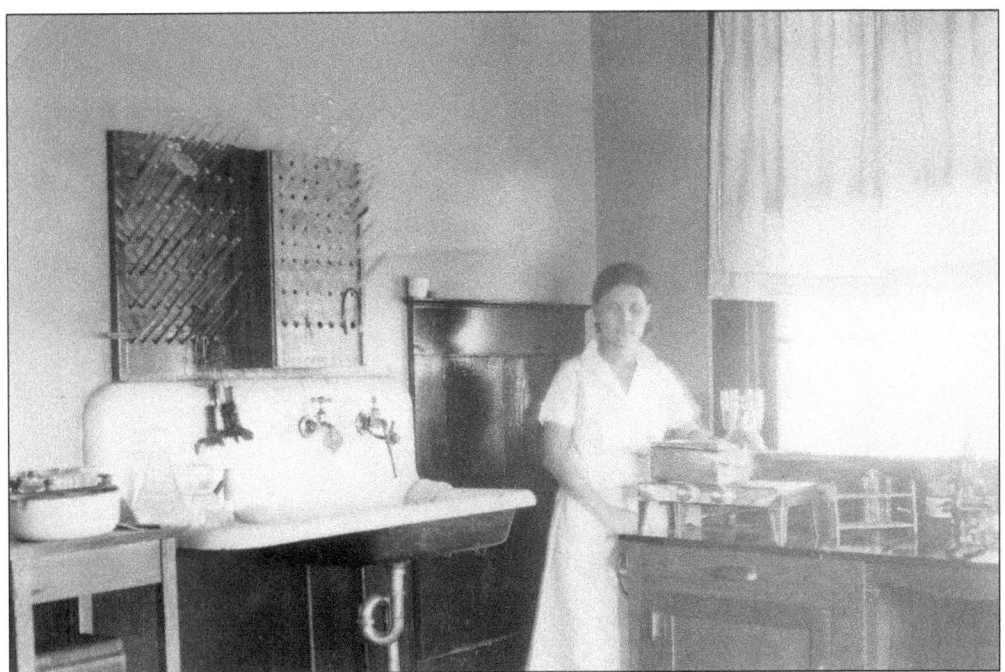

A staff member works in the infirmary's lab. Notable are the test tubes over the sink and the partial view of the microscope on the table. The lab likely could not detect complex illnesses, but it could detect the presence of infections caused by mosquitoes, intestinal parasites, and the like.

The infirmary pharmacy contained bottles of drugs and scales for preparation of medications. A pharmacology text appears on the cabinet. The staff would not have had access to antibiotics because they were not developed until the late 1930s.

A doctor runs a medical test. He holds what appears to be a vial of blood. While the infirmary might not have had access to much of the equipment that larger hospitals had, it nonetheless offered a reasonable standard of care. Both the doctors and nurses had identical credentials to those at larger facilities.

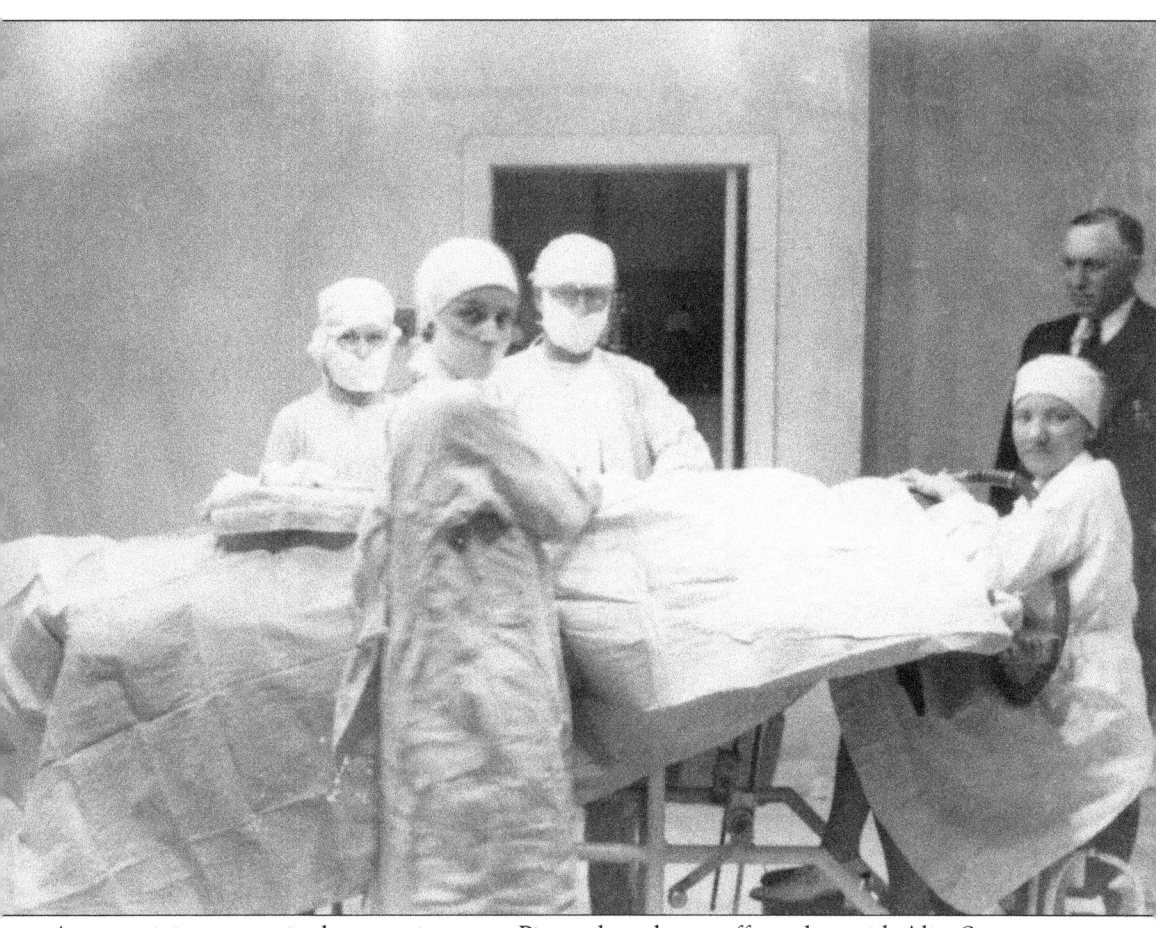

A surgery is in progress in the operating room. Pictured are three staff members with Alice Stewart administering the anesthetic. Also present is a visitor. The most likely surgeries involved wounds, both gunshot and knife, stemming from conflicts among prisoners and the staff. Histories of Parchman report that some knife wounds were self-inflicted. Although the infirmary staff could not have performed complicated procedures because of a lack of more sophisticated equipment, they could take care of broken bones, wounds, injuries resulting from farming accidents like falls from farm machinery, and snake and insect bites. They could also treat colds, flu, food poisoning, and other common ailments. Since Parchman was in an isolated part of Sunflower County, the nearest hospital was at least 10 miles away; it may not have had more advanced medical equipment than Parchman did anyway.

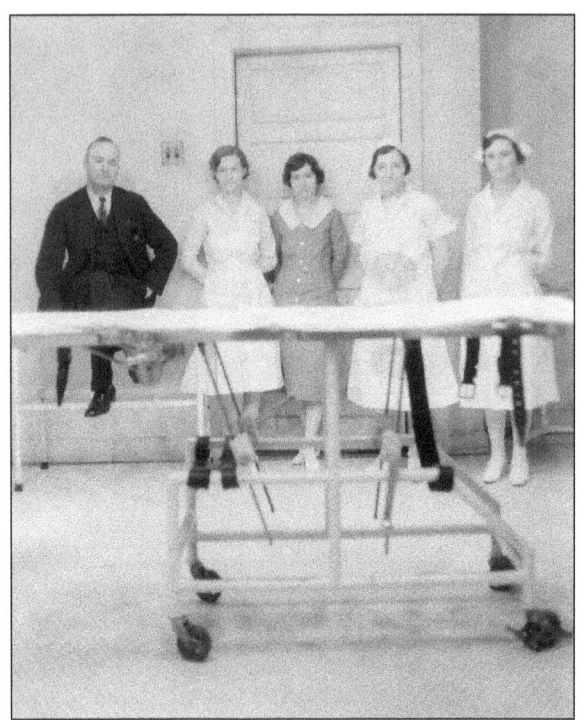

Four staff members stand in the operating room; Alice Stewart is second from the left. The staff were able to perform various operations, such as removal of the appendix and tonsils, and other routine procedures. Patients recuperated in the wards of the infirmary. In the event a patient needed an especially serious surgery, they could have possibly been sent to either Oxford, some 60 miles away, where the University of Mississippi medical school was then located, or to Memphis, which was 80 miles from Parchman.

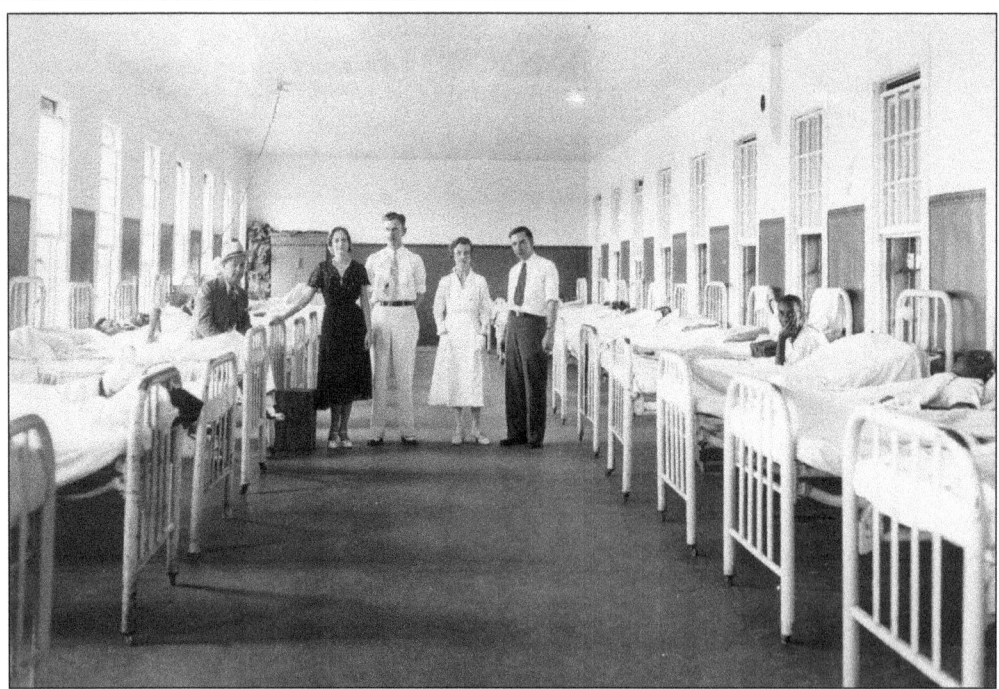

Several staff members and visitors appear in one of the wards. This is the ward for African American prisoners; the infirmary was separated by gender, race, and disease. The two men's wards could have handled 20 patients in each. There were so few woman—no more than 30 in the 1930s—that they had a smaller ward. Parchman remained racially segregated until the late 1960s or early 1970s; it still separates prisoners by gender.

Three members of the nursing staff are pictured at the infirmary; Alice Stewart, head nurse, stands at right. Because of the designation on their caps, they were likely graduate nurses. Stewart had served as a nurse at two veterans' hospitals before arriving at Parchman; she had also taught nursing courses at the Gartley-Ramsey Hospital in Memphis. Newcomers stopped first at the administration building and then went to the infirmary; both buildings were just inside the front gate. The medical staff oversaw physical exams when new prisoners arrived and took Bertillon measurements, which recorded physical characteristics and determined if the new inmates were able to do fieldwork. The staff also fingerprinted and took photographs of the prisoners. The nursing staff oversaw the basic care of the patients by checking temperature and vital signs throughout the day.

A staff nurse stands outside the infirmary. Her spectator pumps are noteworthy as they are not standard nursing footwear. Several photographs of the nurses in street attire show that they kept up with the fashions of the time.

A young man in knickers stands outside the infirmary. He was either the child of a staff member or a visitor. Historians suggest that the visitation policy at Parchman in its earlier days was liberal. The children of prison employees attended school in Drew, a hamlet some eight miles from Parchman.

This head-and-shoulders shot of a nurse may be the official photograph used by the hospital to designate staff members, as several other photographs resemble this one. As with other employees, a nurse had to know a state official, a member of the prison board, or some other politically connected individual to become a member of the hospital staff. In the case of a nurse, the chief of staff at the infirmary would write a formal letter of support, addressed to the governor. The letter would highlight the individual's qualifications for the job.

A nurse stands in front of the infirmary, which was completed around 1917.

Two nurses stand on a front stoop of the infirmary. Alice Stewart is on the left, and the other is unidentified. Stewart's photographs contain an usually large number of infirmary shots. Virtually none of the histories of Parchman contain photographs of the infirmary and staff, including collections housed at the archives department of Mississippi. Because the histories offer so little information on the hospital—amounting to a sentence here and a sentence there—the photographs in this volume contain perhaps the most complete history of medical care at Parchman.

Alice Stewart and her brother John stand in front of the infirmary. In the 1930s, John worked in the post office in Leland, Mississippi, so he could have visited from time to time. During her nine years at Parchman, Alice's family and friends visited occasionally. Before she arrived at Parchman, she had worked at veterans' hospitals in Memphis, Tennessee, and Outwood, Kentucky; she was 32 years old when she arrived at Parchman. The prison was 70 or so miles from her home near New Albany, Mississippi.

A nurse (left) and two individuals pose in front of a screened porch at the infirmary. This long porch appears in the background of several photographs; it would have been helpful for ventilation during the summer months.

A group stands near the infirmary. Alice Stewart is sixth from the left. In the background appears one of the staff houses built for Parchman employees. A nurse might have lived in one of them if she were married. An unmarried nurse would likely live in the infirmary. A water tower appears at right in the background behind other outbuildings. This picture gives insight into the location of the infirmary relative to other facilities.

A doctor does some paperwork. The state legislature expected periodic reports from Parchman detailing expenditures at the infirmary as it was not a revenue producer, and the legislature wanted to ensure that the prison was profitable. Although the medical staff included information about the health of prisoners, the state legislature and governor would not have been as interested in that information.

This group of nurses was photographed in a rose garden in front of the infirmary. Attractive landscaping at Parchman would not have been a top priority for state officials as it did not produce income, but prisoners did work in the gardens.

This is likely a group shot of the infirmary staff. Alice Stewart (far right) is the only one identified.

Pictured is Alice Stewart, who served as head nurse from 1930 to 1939.

Alice Stewart sits in one of the rooms in the infirmary. She was likely on duty in one of the wards.

The infirmary is seen here from a different angle. Although not lavish, the photograph shows that some attention was paid to creating an attractive landscape.

This is a better view of the architectural features of the building. Clearly it was designed for function, not beauty.

Four

WOMEN AND PARCHMAN

At times, people have been prone to make jokes about women in prison. They have sometimes become the fodder for popular entertainment. The reality, though, is that women did populate Parchman in the 1930s as both inmates and support staff. Only 60 women resided as inmates at Parchman, with fewer than 10 of them white women. Apparently, a majority of the female staff members served in the infirmary.

When her husband died in the mid-1920s, Betsy Montgomery was appointed to complete his term as a member of the state's penitentiary board; such appointments are common practices in the South. She was elected to a full term beginning in 1927. Later, she served as president of the board from 1932 to 1936. William Banks Taylor notes that "Miss Betsy" sought to have a penal system that would treat prisoners with compassion (she was particularly concerned about the possibly of heatstroke among those toiling in the fields in summer) and operated Parchman with transparency. She had the help of Gov. Carroll Garten in this endeavor. Betsy Montgomery's humanity may have had effects many would not necessarily imagine. The women who worked at Parchman had a profound effect on the inmates.

A former inmate wrote to Alice Stewart after his release from Parchman: "Miss Stewart, honestly there is no one that appreciates the many courtesies extended to me while I was there . . . taking my post-graduate course . . . any more than I do. You were wonderful to me and I will always have a very warm place in my heart for you. You didn't have to be nice to me, but you did, and that sank deep in my being."

Betsy Montgomery, right, who served on the state board of prisons from 1927 to 1936, is pictured at a hog killing. The men are rendering lard in the black pots. Montgomery's husband was one of Gov. James K. Vardaman's cronies. Vardaman took only a menial interest in the humane treatment of prisoners. He did, though, suggest that they should receive some sort of vocational education. Vardaman did little to institute these educational opportunities. Montgomery did, however, take an active interest in Parchman by visiting more regularly. She also made sure that prisoners had hats, usually pith helmets, as they worked in the fields.

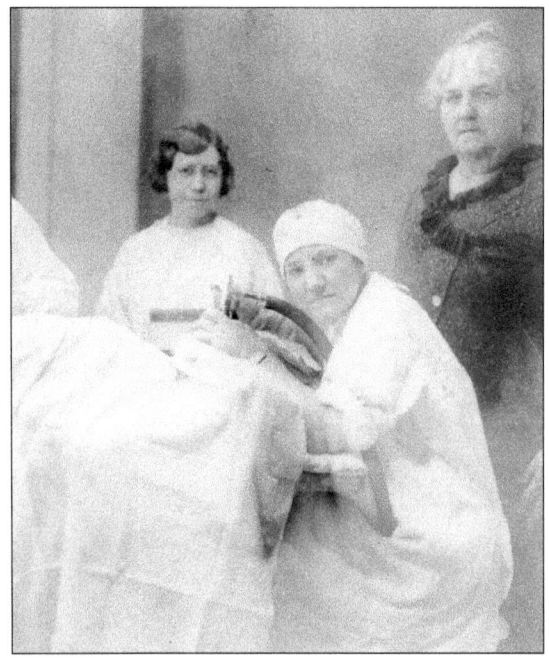

Betsy Montgomery, right, visits the operating room at the infirmary during an inspection around 1933. Alice Stewart, seated, administers the anesthetic. Montgomery was concerned about the health of the prisoners; she was especially concerned about their succumbing to heatstroke as they labored in the fields.

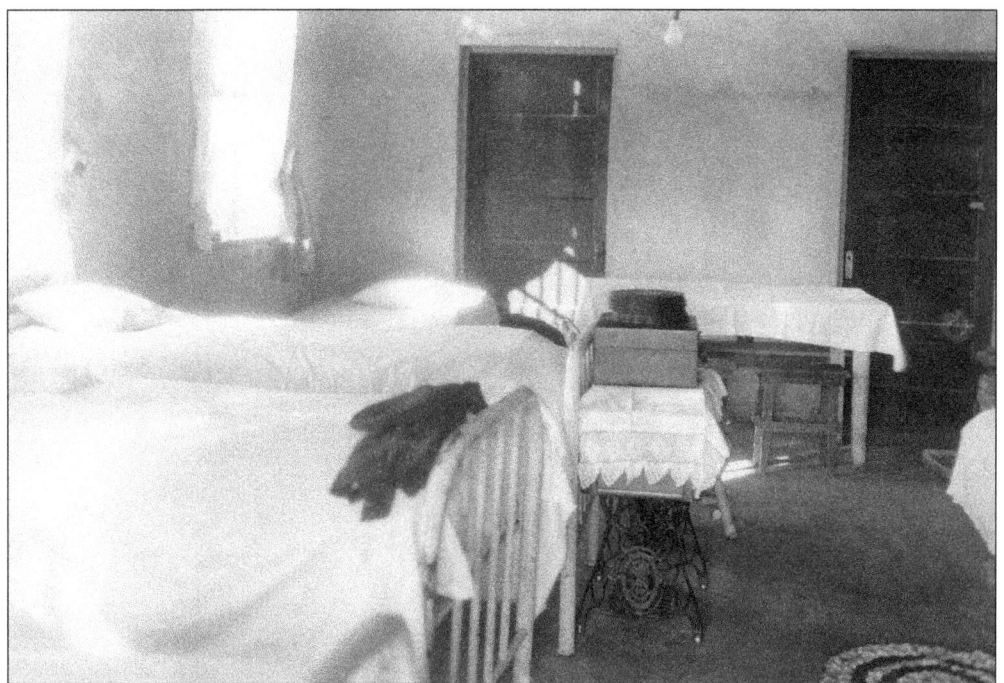

This photograph shows sleeping quarters, but its true purpose is unknown. It may be the quarters for white female prisoners, as fewer than 10 were at Parchman in the 1930s. The room contains a sewing machine and a phonograph, amenities that inmates would not likely have. This may be sleeping quarters for the nurses on the infirmary staff.

The hospital staff gathers outside the infirmary on a snowy day. Alice Stewart is at left; the others are nurses. Interestingly, a doctor appears with them.

A nurse entertains unnamed visitors. Photographic evidence suggests that visitors could call on staff members freely. In the background, prisoners are looking out the windows. Parchman hired few outside employees. The infirmary staff was one of the larger groups.

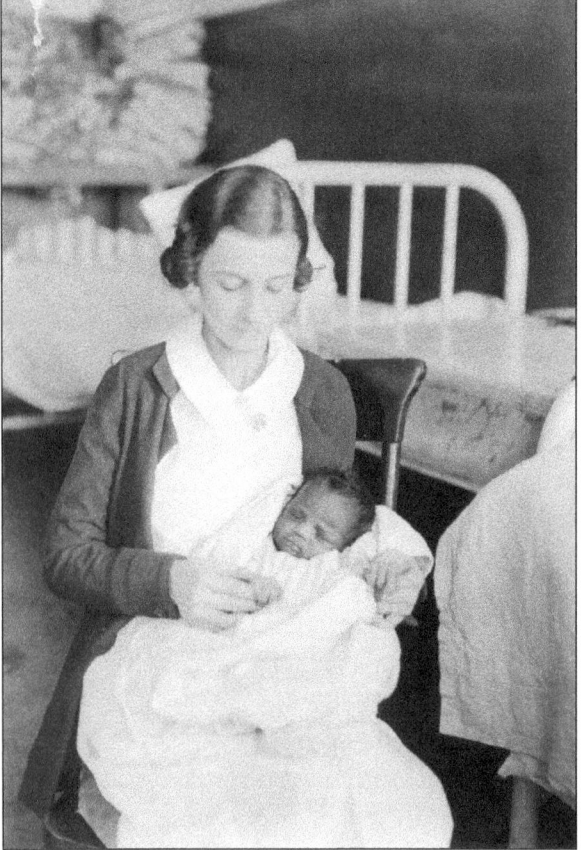

A nurse is pictured with a newborn. The infant likely belonged to one of the prisoners. Parchman allowed conjugal visits for legally married convicts early in its history. The prison was, in fact, a pioneer in allowing visits from spouses. This practice ceased within the last 10 years. Early in its history, Parchman brought in prostitutes. The administration believed that these visits prevented unrest among the inmates. The women did not have this privilege because of the fear of pregnancies.

This photograph was taken outside the infirmary. The woman is unidentified.

Three children play in a swimming pool behind one of the staff houses. Martha Ruth Mauney (second from right), a niece of Alice Stewart, was visiting her aunt (far right) at Parchman.

A nurse sits outside the infirmary with two cats. These felines appear to be household pets as opposed to barn cats, which were around for rodent control. Barn cats were less pampered.

This photograph presents two women and a man on horseback. They are likely in front of a staff house. Leisure activities at Parchman were rather meager. The prisoners did have baseball equipment, but little else. The staff seemingly had a bit more to do when they were not working. They played tennis, rode horses, listened to music, and attended church services at the chapel built for them on the Parchman grounds.

A woman, likely the spouse of a Parchman employee, stands on the front porch of one of the staff cottages. The three prisoners were household help. This supports the notion that Parchman was designed as a postbellum plantation.

This woman was possibly married to one of the higher-ranking prison officials.

Three of the nurses prepare to ride horses. Alice Stewart is in the middle. The horses would have also provided transportation around the grounds and fields for the state-employed guards and farm managers. In addition, Parchman had many mules—at one time around 750—that were used for farming.

Two members of the nursing staff meet for a game of tennis; their shoes seem unfit for recreation. The tennis court is serviceable, not fancy; it did provide a leisure activity for the staff though. It is unknown whether the prisoners had access to this facility.

Alice Stewart watches as a man plays with a squirrel. The building is not identified.

Alice Stewart feeds the squirrel. These images of a pet squirrel seem out of place at a prison, but they indicate that individuals could escape their daily routines.

Five

PARCHMAN AND POPULAR CULTURE

The Mississippi State Penitentiary does not hold quite the same iconic status as Alcatraz, Angola, or Sing Sing, but it has managed to carve out a place in popular culture in film, music, and literature.

The cultural aspects of Parchman emerged when John and Alan Lomax, father and son folklorists and musicologists, visited the prison in 1933 and recorded the songs that the African American inmates sang as they worked in the fields. The elder Lomax worked under the auspices of the Library of Congress. In 1960, Wendell Cannon organized a band composed of prisoners that toured nationally. Photographs from the 1930s, however, prove that the band tradition is a long-standing one. Parchman's musical tradition granted the prison a point of interest along the Mississippi Blues Trail.

Despite its strong presence in the musical world, though, Parchman has achieved greater fame in literature. A number of writers, including John Grisham in *The Chamber*, used the Mississippi State Penitentiary as a backdrop in their fiction. Mink Snopes, one of William Faulkner's iconic characters, served 38 years at Parchman. The world of fiction and reality collided when Faulkner used A.J. "Pap" Tabor as the inspiration for the Tall Convict in *The Wild Palms*. The writer was no doubt inspired by a newspaper article from the 1930s that recounted a birthday celebration of the 90-year-old convicted murderer.

Tabor arrived at Parchman in 1915 to begin a life sentence. By the 1930s, he was no longer physically able to toil in the fields with the other prisoners. Gov. Theodore G. Bilbo first granted the 88-year-old Tabor a pardon in 1932. Tabor declined the offer; a short time later, he again rejected a pardon. Given his age, the prison established an apartment for him in the infirmary. He had a valet who accompanied him on fishing trips, and he would often be seen in the fields bedecked in a three-piece suit. In 1934, the prison staff feted him with a birthday party in honor of his 90th birthday. A newspaper article established him as something of a folk hero.

This group of prisoners, both general population and trusties, were members of a band. Their instruments are largely strings, but they did have percussion, trombone, and alto saxophone. Historians have not mentioned this group of musicians. Perhaps the visit by John and Alan Lomax in 1933 accounts for the band getting lost in the shuffle. The Library of Congress commissioned the father and son team to collect and record blues music in the Southern states. The younger Lomax made several more trips to Parchman, and that collection remains the touchstone of blues music. In the early 1950s, the chaplain at Parchman put together an orchestra composed of prisoners. Later, a prison band took its music on the road and performed at various locations in the region. This little band from the 1930s received no mention.

A.J. "Pap" Tabor, right, is shown with a convict. Sentenced to life for murder, Tabor arrived at Parchman in 1915. In the 1930s, he achieved the status, albeit short-lived, as a folk hero when he rejected pardons from Governors Bilbo and Carroll.

Tabor reads the *Commercial Appeal* (based in Memphis, Tennessee) in the infirmary. As he aged, he could no longer work in the fields. The *Commercial Appeal* was likely the only daily newspaper available at Parchman. Some Mississippi historians have remarked that the state is divided by the newspapers they read: north relied on the Memphis paper; central read the *Clarion-Ledger* or *Jackson Daily News*, both Jackson, Mississippi, papers; and many on the coast, especially in Biloxi, read the *New Orleans Times-Picayune*.

Tabor sits in his apartment in the infirmary, where he could enjoy his pipe and listen to the radio. A feature story described Tabor's apartment as "a well-furnished room." One of the reasons he gave for not leaving Parchman was that he could "have more comfort than any of those rich people down around Biloxi or Jackson. They're worried about the stock market, but I'm not."

Tabor donned a coat and tie after he ceased labor in the fields. Except when he went fishing, his usual attire was a suit. Some photographs show him in jeans, which were seen on prisoners when they labored in the fields.

Tabor (first row, third from right) is pictured with kitchen staff. While no one is sure, Tabor may have lived in this camp before his move to the apartment, and he may have counted these individuals as close friends. He may also have worked in the kitchen, as each camp had its own cooking facility and dining room.

Tabor stands in the middle of a field. The buildings in the background are unidentified. Given the number of photographs of Tabor in the Stewart collection, one wonders if the photographer staged this picture.

Tabor, at far left, enjoyed fishing in his leisure time. His valet, Ed, second from left, holds the catch of the day. Ed would bait Pap's hook on fishing trips. The two men on the right are unidentified. A Baltimore newspaper mentioned Tabor and highlighted his rejecting two pardons. It also included information on Ed, the prison trusty who served as his valet.

Here, Tabor holds his birthday cake as he celebrates his 90th birthday. The newspaper article that gave "Pap" his 15 minutes of fame mentioned the "real party" that the prison staff held for him.

Tabor was honored for his 90th birthday with a party. Fellow convicts, relatives, and prison staff joined him for the celebration. A newspaper wire story covered the event and recounted Pap's rejection of two pardons. Because of that article, William Faulkner was inspired to use Tabor as the inspiration for one of his characters.

BIBLIOGRAPHY

Mississippi Department of Archives and History. www.mdah.ms.gov//arrec/digital_archives/

Oshinsky, David M. *"Worse Than Slavery:" Parchman Farm and the Ordeal of Jim Crow Justice.* New York, NY: Simon & Schuster, 1996.

Taylor, William Banks. *Down on Parchman Farm.* Columbus, OH: Ohio State University Press, 1999.

Visit us at
arcadiapublishing.com

www.ingramcontent.com/pod-product-compliance
Lightning Source LLC
Chambersburg PA
CBHW060939170426
43194CB00027B/2998